Affectio... ...ying ...e
Power of Death:

Wills, Probate & Death Duty Records

Jane Cox

Federation of Family History Societies

Published by
The Federation of Family History Societies (Publications) Ltd
2-4 Killer Street, Ramsbottom, Bury,
Lancashire BL0 9BZ

First published 1993
Reprinted 1995
Reprinted 1998

ISBN 1 872094 68 6

Printed and bound by Oxuniprint, Great Clarendon Street, Oxford OX2 6DP

For Yvonne

In *Sketches by Boz,* Charles Dickens described the probate records he knew from his time as a legal clerk as 'the records of old likings and dislikings' and of 'affection defying the power of death'.

Thomas Cullwicke of St Anne and St Agnes, Aldersgate left everything to his wife:

'All that I have I give unto thee and am sorye that it is no more.'

SEARCHING FOR WILLS.

INTERIOR OF THE PREROGATIVE WILL OFFICE, DOCTORS' COMMONS.

CONTENTS

ABOUT THIS BOOKLET

Wills and probate records are, after census returns, parish registers and the registers of births, marriages and deaths, the most important source material for family historians.

They are also invaluable for the study of local history, social and economic history, and biography, and are fascinating for anyone who is intrigued by the past.

This book is an introduction to the use of these documents for amateur historians of all sorts, with the family historian primarily in mind.

The questions listed below are some of those which will be considered.

Did your ancestor leave a will?

Why are there so few women's wills?

What is a grant of administration?

Where can you read the will or administration?

What is the difference between a will and a testament and what is meant by real and personal estate?

What does a will contain and what does it mean?

How much money did your ancestor leave?

What other documentation might survive?

Why are Death Duty Records useful?

INTRODUCTION

In England and Wales wills survive for a wide range of people, gentlemen, merchants, shopkeepers, farmers; even humble labourers and artisans have occasionally left some account of themselves. Some were written as long ago as the middle ages. They, and the related probate and death duty documents, are potentially the most exciting and fruitful records that the historian of an ordinary family has at his disposal

Unless by some fortunate chance letters or diaries have survived, which only applies to the literate sections of society, the will may be the only place where personal details are to be found. As well as naming relatives and enabling vital links to be made for the family tree, the will invariably gives clues to a man's status and occupation and bequests of treasured possessions may suggest interests and hobbies.

More than that, some, when dictating their last wishes, open their hearts, making confessions perhaps, like George Hulm, an oilman of The Strand who died in 1813. His greatest sin was pissing in the ink horns when he was at school!

Some testators express loves and hates which might otherwise have been locked up for posterity. Charles Dickens described wills and their associated documents, with which he had some acquaintance when working as a legal clerk, as the records of 'old likings and dislikings', of 'affection defying the power of death' and of 'hatred pursued beyond the grave'. Wills can be windows into men's souls. The exiled James II, sadly wise after the event, told his son in his will, 'A king can never be happy unless his subjects be easy'.

DID YOUR ANCESTOR LEAVE A WILL?

Before the present century, a fairly small percentage of the adult male population left wills which went through the process of being authorised or 'proved' in a court of law. Women are represented very scantily in the will registers; most of them are rich widows. There may have been many more wills left that we have no knowledge of, as those we have access to are the records which went through the legal process of probate.

When Tony Weller's wife died in *Pickwick Papers* she left a will in a tea pot on the mantelpiece. Tony was all for putting it on the fire, as he said to his son Sam, 'As it's all right and satisfactory to you and me as is the only parties interested'. Sam was unusually informed about the law for an ordinary working man of his time, and insisted that they should 'Get a probe of this here'.

There must have been many such instances. There was no statutory requirement for any legal proceeding, to be gone through when someone died, as regards to his or her estate, until 1815. And even after that the law was never rigorously applied. It was left, as it is now, to those who had an interest in the dead man's money or property to take action. These days a bank, building society or insurance company asks for a grant of probate (the legal certificate which gives the stamp of authority to the will) before releasing a dead man's money. In the past there were organisations and individuals for whom a grant of probate might be needed. A solicitor's widow, for instance, would need to produce legal documentation to claim her husband's back pay.

In many cases, however, the occasion did not arise and nobody bothered to 'get a probe of this here'. The number of wills that were tossed into the fire or left in the drawer where they were found cannot be counted and does not concern us here.

In the majority of cases, when the farm labourers, textile workers or factory hands who constituted most of the population died, whatever cash there was in the house was taken by the widow or children who would also apply to the local lord of the manor to have the property title transferred into their name. Maybe the dying man had told the curate, or whoever was in attendance, that he wanted his eldest son to have his blunderbuss and his godson to have his pewter tankard. The blunderbuss and the tankard would be duly presented and, unless it looked as if there might be a fight over who was entitled to what, no one would bother to go to the trouble and expense of any legal fiddle faddle.

Various categories of people were barred from will making; excommunicants, sodomites, usurers and libellers were among them and there were restrictions for married women (see below, p. 9). The wills of criminals, outlaws and lunatics were thrown out. If it could be shown, however, that a lunatic had expressed his last wishes during a period of lucidity or before he went mad, then they would be considered by the courts.

Wills made by boys under fourteen and girls under twelve were invalid. The law recognised, long ago, that girls reach maturity before boys! In order to leave land legally, both male and female had to be twenty-one. (The question of landed property is discussed more fully on pages 20 and 22.)

You might think that as time went by an increasing number of people left wills. In fact, relatively more people seem to have left proven wills in the fifteenth and early sixteenth centuries than was the case later, although survival is patchy. Before the Reformation, the Church brought a great deal of pressure to bear as regards the disposal of a dying man's money. Your parish priest might tell you that to die intestate (without making a will) was as bad as dying unshriven. It has been suggested that in the fifteenth century as many as 70 per cent of men left wills, including cooks, gardeners, gravediggers and herdsmen.

By the late seventeenth century the situation seems to have changed. In London, at least, evidence suggests that, among the ordinary folk perhaps as few as 2 per cent left wills which went to probate. As might be expected, the wealthier your ancestor the more chance you have of finding a will for him. In the reign of William and Mary about a quarter of the male residents of the salubrious parish of St Anne's Westminster left wills.

For the great mass of the Victorian labouring poor there is little trace in the probate records. In the present century about 60 per cent of the population (men and women) leave wills and for about 15 per cent grants of administration are made.

WHY ARE THERE SO FEW WOMEN'S WILLS?

Very few wills of married women are to be found before the present century. If you come across a will for an ancestress, she is probably a widow. Most spinsters had little to leave.

There were restrictions as to what a married woman could legally own. Before the Married Women's Property Act came in to force in 1883, *femes coverts,* as they were known, were technically barred from landowning, although there were ways round the law and many private arrangements were made through marriage settlements.

In the vast majority of cases, however, when a wife died there was no need for any formality to be gone through. Everything belonged to her husband.

As far as widows were concerned, the husband's will, if he left one, would normally have given his wife a life interest in his estate, leaving the assets ultimately to the children or other heirs. You will find exceptions to this, of course. There are wills for some wealthy, independent widows.

From the early middle ages there were repeated attempts to render the wills of married women illegal. The dying Catherine of Aragon, spurned wife of Henry VIII, refusing to admit that she was divorced to the last, got her physician to write a 'little bill . . . knowing according to English law a wife can make no will'.

Catherine was not quite right. The Church had managed to salvage some women's rights and a wife was allowed to bequeath her personal savings, property given her for her own separate use, pin money, maintenance, and any assets which were 'in action', such as money she had in hand as executrix or administratrix of somebody else. She might also be empowered to make a will under the terms of her marriage settlement. Her husband had to approve the contents of the will and the appointment of an executor. He was also entitled to take out letters of administration (see below) as to that part of his wife's estate over which she had no rights of disposal. Most husbands did not bother.

WHAT IS A GRANT OF ADMINISTRATION?

If it was necessary or useful for someone to establish their rights in law over a dead man's belongings and no will could be found, then the claimant, usually the widow or next-of-kin, might apply to the court for letters of administration (abbreviated to 'admon' in the records).

The person who reckoned they had the greatest claim on the estate, after waiting for fourteen days to elapse from the death, applied to the court, usually through a local lawyer, and simply took an oath. No proof of death or kinship was normally required; according to one lawyer 'no questions were asked'. The formalities were usually completed within two months.

The claimant was then appointed the official administrator of the estate and was issued with a small parchment document bearing the seal of the court. That authorised him or her to share out the assets according to whatever the rules of distribution were at that date.

Unless there was a great deal of money involved or a dispute was on the cards or a legal title was required for some particular purpose, people rarely bothered to go through the procedure of taking out letters of administration. If, for instance, the deceased happened to have been a legatee under somebody else's will, then his widow would need to apply for an administration in order to get hold of that legacy.

Letters of administration in the goods of Gilbert Meese of St Paul's, Covent Garden, granted by the Prerogative Court of Canterbury in 1665 (Public Record Office PROB 32/1/62). The administration form was in Latin until the mid-eighteenth century.

11

Richus Swifte
ad de bonis
comiss' mensis
Martii 1617

Decimo quarto die emanavit comissio
Francisce Swift relte Richi Swift nuper
parochie beate Marie Magdalene in
Barmondsey in Com Surr' des' hentes etc.
ad administranda bona iura et credita
dci des' de bene etc. in persona Richi
Goodall notarii public procuris sui etc.
iurat'

Winton

Ascensio
Inventarium
exhibitum xxj

Blasii Computavit

12

Richard Swifte admon. of goods unadministered granted March 1617/8

On the fourteenth day {of March} a commission issued to Frances Swift the relict of Richard Swift late of the parish of the Blessed Magdalene in Bermondsey in the county of Surrey deceased having etc. {whilst he lived and at the time of his death goods etc. sufficient to found the jurisdiction of the Prerogative Court} to administer the goods rights and credits of the said deceased she being sworn truly to administer in the person of her proctor, Richard, notary public

Winchester diocese

Inventory to be exhibited by Ascension; exhibited on {March} 21st

Account to be returned by the feast of St Blaise (February); {administrator} has accounted

Top, entry in the Prerogative Court of Canterbury Administration Act Book for March 1599 concerning the intestate estate of Richard Swift (Public Record Office PROB 6/ 6 f. 9). Below are shown a transcription and a translation of the entry.

It was fairly common for a dead man's creditors, or the chief one, to take administration of his estate, that being the surest way of getting paid.

If your ancestor left a widow, she would normally be the person assigned to look after his assets. But, as a lawyer's manual of 1702 advised 'It is the fear of many to administer, especially of widows; yet, without doubt it is the best and safest way'. The more timorous widow might turn the job over to a brother or friend, executing 'letters of renunciation'.

Next choice to the widow was next-of-kin. Technically the widow could not be described as next-of-kin as she was not a blood relative. It was often your ancestor's local attorney who made the effective choice of administrator, notifying the court and obtaining its sanction. It was not unusual for clergymen to be appointed to look after a parishioner's assets and masters of merchant vessels were often chosen to deal with anything left by an apprentice who died on board.

Until the late seventeenth century, the court might take over administration itself. This practice was known as either 'distribution' or 'limitation'. Under Cromwell, when the church courts' probate activities were centralised in one London Court of Probate, about one third of all estates were subject to distribution orders.

Grants of administration have never been as common as probated wills and there is, therefore, less chance of finding one for an ancestor. If you do find one, the surviving documentation usually provides scant information, just the names and addresses of the deceased and the next-of-kin and a date. It may be an entry in a register or the bond the administrator was required to enter into.

If it is the latter, then you will be able to get some idea of the value of the estate in question as the bond was related to that value. The amount of security required was either roughly equivalent to the value of the estate or double it. You will also get the name of the person who stood security with the administrator, who may have been a relative.

You should bear in mind that the dead man's real property, his freehold and copyhold land, was not included in the valuation for the bond.

How was the dead man's money shared out? The main statutory basis for the share out was the Statute of Distributions of 1670, which stipulated that the widow should have one third and that the residue should be divided equally between the children or whatever other relatives stood as next-of-kin. The dead man's real estate was a different matter and was governed by different rules. This is explained on pages 20 and 22.

The statute more or less put existing practise on a firm legal footing. The only real difference from the situation which pertained previously was that the heir-at-law (the eldest son, usually, who inherited the landed property) was now allowed an equal share in the money with his brothers and sisters.

The estates of married women went *in toto* to their husbands.

If there was no spouse or children, then the parents of the deceased had first claim, followed by remoter relatives. If no relatives turned up or none could be found then the money would go to the crown, in theory at least. Lawyers regularly put advertisements in newspapers in an attempt to trace beneficiaries. Often someone such as a landlady or the person who had nursed the dying man might apply to the Treasury Solicitor for money which had escheated; such an application was almost always well received.

A whole variety of special or limited grants of administration could be obtained to deal with differing circumstances. If the next-of-kin was a child, for instance, the grant would be made to someone else until he or she became of age. If it was known that there was a will somewhere but nobody could find it, then a temporary grant of administration might be made until it turned up or was obtained from abroad. All the different sorts are described in *Wills, Inventories and Death Duties* by Jane Cox (Public Record Office, 1988, pp. 16—22).

In the original contemporary church court annual indexes or calendars, administrations are often in a separate section following the wills. Even in the printed indexes for the Principal Probate Registry (Somerset House) from 1858, they are separated until 1870, though combined thereafter. Many local record offices now have modern indexes, compiled for the historical researcher, to probate records in their keeping. Often these are to the wills only, as the less informative administrations have a low priority. Nevertheless, it is always worth asking for administration indexes as they are sometimes neglected or forgotten.

WHERE CAN YOU READ THE WILL OR ADMINISTRATION?

From January 1858

All wills proved and administrations granted in England and Wales from this date can be read in the Principal Probate Registry at

Somerset House in London. There are clear alphabetical indexes on open bookshelves and a very small fee is charged to consult the wills, which are produced for you within a very short time. Photocopies are cheap and will be posted to you within a few days.

The staff shout out the name of the testator (the person who made the will) in a loud voice and you go to collect a fat register with a will entered in it. Thus the only slight problem in this most straightforward research operation occurs if you are researching a very odd-sounding or foreign surname. You may have difficulty recognising what is called out.

Somerset House is in the Strand, to the east of Waterloo Bridge. The telephone number is 071 936 7000 and the search rooms are open Monday to Friday from 10 a.m. to 4.30 p.m. You will need to take a pencil.

Postal enquiries, which are dealt with normally within 21 days, should be sent to The Chief Clerk, York Probate Sub-Registry, Duncombe Place, York YO1 2EA. The fee charged for searching and supplying a photocopy of a will is £2 to include postage (at the time of writing).

District probate hold microfiche indexes of all wills proved from 1973 to date and copies of wills proved locally.

The Society of Genealogists has microfilm copy of the will and administration calendars, 1858—1930. The films are also held by some Mormon libraries.

Sets of the printed Indexes of Grants are located (as of Autumn 1988) as follows, in some cases including a few years later than those indicated:

Avon:	Bristol Record Office, 1858—1900.
Beds.:	County Record Office, 1901—1935.
Cambs.:	County Record Office (Cambs. C.C.), Cambridge 1858—1934.
Ches.:	Cheshire Record Office, 1858—1929.
Cornwall:	Bodmin Sub-Registry, Market Street, Bodmin PL31 2VW (Tel. 0208 72279); for eventual transfer to the Cornwall Record office, Truro.
Cumbria:	Cumbria Record Office, Carlisle, 1858—1928.
Devon:	Exeter Sub-Registry, 94 Fore Street, Exeter EX4 3HZ (Tel. 0392 74515).
Glos.:	Gloucestershire Record Office, 1858—1929.
Gtr. Manchester:	Greater Manchester Record Office, 56 Marshall Street, New Cross, Manchester M4 5FU (Tel. 061 832 5284).

Hants. :	Hampshire Record Office, Winchester, 1858—1932.
Lancs. :	Lancashire Record Office, Preston, 1858—1928.
Leics. :	Leicestershire Record Office, 1858—1886 (not in main record office, prior notice required); Leicester Probate Registry, Government Buildings, Newarke Street, Leicester LE1 5SE, 1887 on.
Lincs. :	Lincolnshire Archives Office, 1858—1933.
Merseyside :	Liverpool Record Office, 4th Floor, Brown Picton and Hornby Libraries, William Brown Street, Liverpool, 1858—1928.
Norfolk :	Norwich Local Studies Library, 1858—1937.
Northants. :	see Cambridgeshire.
Notts. :	Nottinghamshire Record Office, 1858—1928.
Oxon. :	Bodleian Library, Oxford (Lower Reading Room, Radcliffe Camera, on open shelves. Readers ticket necessary; daily charge).
East Sussex :	East Sussex Record Office, Lewes, 1858—1928.
West Midlands :	Birmingham Reference Library (Archives Department), 1858—1937.
North Yorks. :	York Sub-Registry, Duncombe Place, York YO1 2EA (Tel. 0904 624210).
South Yorks. :	Sheffield Record Office, Sheffield Central Library, 1858—1928 (prior notice required; no public access, short searches undertaken by staff).
West Yorks. :	West Yorkshire County Record Office, Wakefield, 1858—1928.
Clwyd :	Clwyd Record Office, Ruthin, 1858—1928.
Dyfed :	National Library of Wales, Aberystwyth, 1858—1972.Dyfed Archives, Carmarthen, 1858—1928.
Glamorgan :	Glamorgan Record Office, Cardiff, 1858—1928 (from Llandaff).
Gwynedd :	Gwynedd Archives Service, Caernarfon, 1858—1929 (from Bangor).

Pre-January 1858

Before 1858 there were a whole variety of different courts where wills were proved, most of them belonging to the Church.

Accordingly, those wills are now scattered in different record offices and libraries and there is no comprehensive central index.

The F.F.H.S. publishes an exceilent guide telling you where to go to find wills and what indexes are available, i.e. *Probate Jurisdictions: Where to Look for Wills* by J.S.W. Gibson (formerly called *A Simplified Guide to Probate Jurisdictions*), 4th edn., 1993.

Two earlier and larger books, now out of print but available in good reference libraries and record offices, give considerably more detail. Gibson's *Wills and Where to Find Them* (Phillimore and the British Record Society, 1974) is effectively replaced by his later Guide. A.J. Camp's *Wills and Their Whereabouts* (the author, 4th edn., 1974) is undoubtedly the most informative and authoritative, though not as straightforward for the beginner. So many indexes have been compiled (and often published) in the past twenty years that, whilst details of the actual probate records remain largely unchanged, those to finding aids are now seriously out of date.

There are over 300 probate courts. The system was, essentially, that the wills of ordinary folk had to be taken to the local archdeacon's court. It was the place where a man died, not his home address, which determined the court to which his will went. If the deceased had personal property (the difference between personal and real property is described on p. 20) in more than one archdeaconry, then his estate was dealt with by the bishop's court. If he was in possession of what was known as *bona notabilia* (goods and cash over the value of £5, £10 in London) in more than one diocese, then his will went to the court of the Archbishop of Canterbury, if he lived in the south, or to the court of the Archbishop of York, if he lived in the northern province.

If he had goods in both provinces, then there were supposed to have been grants of probate made in both. If, then, a rich Londoner had shares in a northern railway company, for instance, his will had to go to the Prerogative Court of York and to the Prerogative Court of Canterbury.

As well as the network of courts described above, there were a number of other courts which had a 'peculiar jurisdiction'. This meant that in some areas there was a special probate court attached, perhaps, to the local parish church, usually a hang-over from pre-Reformation days when the local monastery had held a court. In Witham Friary in Somerset, for instance, the local farmers had their wills proved by the parish priest who was the 'heir' to the Carthusian monastery which had once ruled the village.

The deans and chapters of cathedrals had probate jurisdiction over the cathedral close and villages that belonged to them.

In addition there were a number of manorial courts which had acquired the right to prove the wills of people who died on the manor.

The search for wills should start in the appropriate diocesan record office, which is usually, though not always, the same as the county record office, where you may find the wills of ordinary people. The wealthier members of society may have had wills proved in the courts of the provinces of the two archbishops.

The records of the court for the southern province, the Prerogative Court of Canterbury (PCC) are in the Public Record Office's Chancery Lane building (London WC2A 1LR Tel. 081 876 3444 and ask for the Rolls Room). The records of the Court of the Province of York are at the Borthwick Institute of Historical Research, St. Anthony's Hall, Peaseholme Green, York YO1 2PW (Tel. 0904 59861 ext 274).

The Prerogative Court of Canterbury, which sat in London, greatly expanded its business over the years. Only there was a skilled bar and bench, and the Bank of England decided in 1810 that, as far as they were concerned, the only grant of probate which counted was a PCC grant. What with that and inflation (£5 was a great deal in 1500 and not so much by 1700) the PCC took an increasing number of wills from all over the country. For the researcher, that means that certainly by the nineteenth century, quite humble testators are to be found in the PCC, including the author's great great grandfather who was a milkman in Bethnal Green.

Even in earlier times, this was not uncommon, especially amongst dissenters such as Quakers not wanting to have dealings with local ecclesiastical authorities. It is much too easily and wrongly assumed that PCC was confined to the landed classes and the very wealthy. In contrast, in the period 1571–1640, almost a fifth of the executors in the small market town of Banbury proved wills in PCC rather than the local peculiar court.

Anyone who died abroad had to have their estate handled by the Prerogative Court of Canterbury, including sailors and soldiers. The PCC will indexes for the sixteenth and seventeenth centuries, which have been published by the British Record Society, are a good way of tracing those emigrants to North America who still had possessions at home.

1653—1660

During the Commonwealth and Protectorate all wills were proved and all grants of administration made at one central Court of Probate in London, which was really the Prerogative Court of Canterbury under a different name. The original records are among those of the PCC in the Public Record Office and there are published indexes to them (British Record Society).

Less people than usual bothered with the legal procedure of probate during this time; it was more expense and trouble to get a grant from London than to go along to the local registry. Nevertheless, the will and administration indexes for this period are an invaluable means of tracking ancestors down. For those few years there *is* one central index for all wills and administrations.

WHAT IS THE DIFFERENCE BETWEEN A WILL AND TESTAMENT AND WHAT IS MEANT BY REAL AND PERSONAL ESTATE?

Most modern wills start 'This is the last will and testament of A'. Strictly speaking a will (*ultima voluntas* in Latin) is a document which contains devise of real estate. Real estate comprised freehold property and property held from the lord of the manor known as copyhold. The document which deals with bequest of personal estate (leases, cash, goods, animals etc) is called a testament. In the middle ages two separate documents were often drawn. Later on this ceased, but the laws governing the two sorts or property and the inheritance of them were quite different.

By the sixteenth century wills and testaments were usually amalgamated into one document, but the church probate courts, which operated until 1858, had no powers over devise of real estate and the probate granted by them only applied to the 'testament part' of the will.

There was, surprisingly, absolutely no provision for probate of wills as regards real property. If any question arose as to the descent of real property, then it was dealt with by the king's court, often the court of Chancery.

Any mention of real property which you may find among the records of the church courts is incidental and any totals or estate valuations which you find in the ecclesiastical records excludes freehold and copyhold property.

This does not apply to probate records after 1858, nor does it apply to Death Duty records from 1853.

Devise of land may be referred to in the will proved in the church court, but not necessarily so and, even if it is, the fact that the will

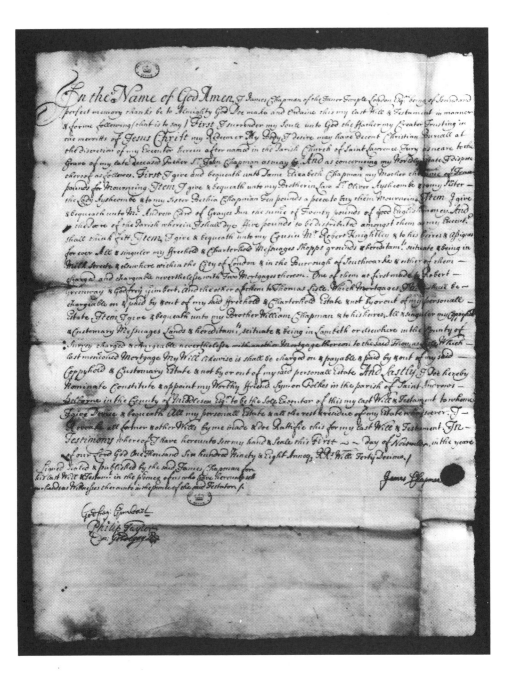

An original will, that of James Chapman, 1696.

was proved does not mean that Rose Cottage did, in fact, go to 'my beloved son, Walter'; there may have been local laws or entails which prevented this happening.

From the thirteenth to the sixteenth century, men were not allowed to leave their real estate to anybody except their natural 'heir-at-law'. There were various ways of getting round this and one favoured method was to convey the land to trustees for the life of the 'owner' for his own use and then to the uses which he set down in his will.

Laws passed in the 1660s permitted devise of land, unless it was entailed (see below).

Most ordinary people's houses were held in copyhold tenure from the lord of the manor. When the tenant died the custom was, in most places, that the widow stayed in the cottage having 'free bench' until she died or remarried. At her death the eldest or youngest son (customs varied) applied to the manorial court to have the property transferred to his name. It might be a daughter if there were no sons.

Under the terms of the 1837 Wills Act copyhold property became devisable and the form of tenure was abolished completely in 1922.

As far as freehold property was concerned, although there was theoretical free devise from the mid-seventeenth century, a will which disinherited the heir might be disputed. From this time, also, entails became increasingly popular. By the mid-eighteenth century one half of all land was entailed and by 1848, the proportion was said to be two thirds.

An entail was set up by a private deed which established the line of descent of property for generations to come. Thus Shakespeare settled his landed property on his elder daughter and her children, grandchildren and so on down. It might be done by will or marriage settlement.

If your ancestor's farm, therefore, had been entailed by his grandfather, for instance, he would have no power to dispose of it when he died and there may be no reference to it in his will.

Tracing the descent of freehold land can be difficult. Your best bet is to consult the deed indexes which most county record offices hold. For the counties of Middlesex and Yorkshire there are deeds registries held locally.

Copyhold is more straightforward as there may be manorial records which survive. To find out where the records for your manor are, you should consult the Manorial Register at the National Register of Archives at Quality House, Quality Court, Chancery Lane, London WC2A 1HF.

WHAT DOES A WILL CONTAIN AND WHAT DOES IT MEAN?

The document which will be produced for you to read in the record office (and certainly at Somerset House) is often not the original document signed by your ancestor, but the court copy of the will which was made at the time of probate and bound up in a register. These copies are known as 'registered copy wills'. They are easily distinguished from the original documents by the fact that the signatures are in the same hand writing as the text. You may have to read them on microfilm.

If you are interested to inspect the signature of your ancestor and those of the people who witnessed the will, you can ask to see the 'original will'.

Most wills start off with a standard preamble: 'In the name of God Amen (In Die nomine Amen), I, Jane Cox being weak in body but of sound and disposing mind, commit my body to etc. etc.'. The soul was then committed to God; Roman Catholic wills often include a prayer for the intercession of the Virgin Mary and puritans were inclined to ask for their souls to be 'washed' or 'cleansed'. Not all preambles are taken from formularies. Dr. Johnson wrote a heartfelt: 'I leave to God a soul polluted with many sins'.

Instructions for burial and funeral arrangements may follow; the older the will, the more likely that specific instructions are to be found. The pre-Reformation preoccupation with the trappings of burial tended to replace, in later wills, by a simple direction that a decent burial should be made at the executor's discretion and at the expense of the estate. Some, like the widow Dolman of St Giles in the Fields, who died in 1650, gave consideration to their 'wake'. She directed that, 'All my friends and acquaintances and loveinge Neighbours bee invited to accompany my Corpes to the grave And bee served with Naples Biskett and Wyne in a competent and comelie sorte, as is in like cases used'. Naples biscuit, the seventeenth century equivalent of malt loaf, was standard fare at funerals.

Much as now, there were formularies which the local lawyer followed when drawing a will for his clients. One of the standard forms included the words 'being somewhat crazy in body', an indication of the prevalence of arthritis.

Those that start with the words 'Memorandum quod' are spoken or nuncupative wills. They are not signed by the testator. Before the law was changed in 1837 spoken wills constituted almost one third of all that went to probate.

Before the present century it was unusual for anyone (except Quakers) to make a will, until they were 'pinched by the messengers of death', unless they were going on some perilous exploit, like a journey abroad. It was something which was done on the death bed, and often it was an informal utterance. The dying man might gasp out his last wishes and, as long as there were three witnesses, then the written version of what he had said stood up in law.

When Nell Gwynne was dying, propped up on pillows in her great silver bed, decorated with cupids, she suddenly remembered one 'Orange Nan' and decided she wanted to leave her £5. Her chaplain scribbled this and other last minute bequests down on the back of a letter and what he wrote was submitted to the court as a nuncupative codicil (afterthought) to Nell's will.

As long as it could be shown that the piece of paper presented to the court truly represented the deceased's intentions, the actual form of it did not matter. Lawyers advised that it was best not to leave matters to the 'slippery memory of witnesses', but many did. If the piece of paper was not a proper will, unsigned and without the required number of witnesses, then affidavits would have to be produced. These were sworn statements about the dead man's wishes and are usually attached to the original will.

Wills proved from 1 January 1838 were governed by the Wills Act passed in the previous year. They now had to be in writing, signed by the testator on every page and attested by at least two witnesses. This did not mean, however, that informally expressed last wishes were now discounted, but there would have to be a full 'propounding' or 'proof in solemn form' before they could be accepted as a true will (see below).

It is very rare for wills to be written by the dying man himself, unless he was a clergyman. Usually a local attorney or scrivener was summoned to the house and given verbal instructions. He would then go away and draw up a document, often using a form from a will manual, bring it back and read it through to the testator. It would then be signed by him and two or more witnesses.

Humble folk might dictate their wishes to the parson or curate who was probably in attendance at the death bed and might be the only literate person around.

The handwriting of the original will is, more often than not, that of the attorney's clerk or scrivener. Do not get too excited thinking the seal of the will is your ancestor's seal, it is often an attorney's seal. You cannot even be too sure about the signature! Before the 1676 Statute of Frauds it was not uncommon for the lawyer to 'forge' the signature on wills, especially if the testator was too ill to hold a quill.

Wills were witnessed by whoever happened to be in the house, servants, relatives or lawyers' clerks. Not until the 1837 Wills Act was it illegal for a beneficiary to witness a will.

If the will maker wanted to add something or make a change at any point after the will had been executed (signed and witnessed) then he could add a 'postscript' which is known as a codicil. It appears in the registered copy as a separate item, signed and witnessed, entered in the register after the text of the main body of the will.

The paragraph at the bottom of the will which is in Latin (until 1733) is known as the 'probate'. It simply states that the will was proved by the oath of the executor, who is named, and gives the date on which this was done and the name of the official who presided. Quaker wills are easily recognisable as they were unable to swear an oath; the probate clause will say that the executor 'affirmed'.

No will could be proved (made legal) unless someone took the responsibility for carrying out its provisions. This was normally the executor or executrix appointed by the deceased. He or she was usually named in the will and a straightforward of 'common form' probate involved nothing more than the court officials' checking through the document to see if it seemed reasonable and was duly signed and witnessed. The executor then took an oath whereby he or she promised to carry out the terms of the will. They did not have to go to court to do it; a commission might be issued which enabled them to take the oath in the presence of some local lawyers or clergy.

Probate usually took a couple of months. If there were complications it might be delayed and when searching for a will it is advisable to go through the indexes for two or three years after the date of death.

From the seventeenth century the vast majority of married men appointed their wives as executrices; it was the best way of guarding their entitlement to a share of the estate. Some widows were nervous about the business side of things and might 'renounce' in favour of a male relative. If the estate in question was large and complicated a lawyer might be named as executor. It was quite usual to have two or more executors and in the sixteenth to eighteenth centuries testators often appointed, in addition, 'overseers' or 'supervisors'. Overseers were entrusted with the task of making sure the deceased's goods were kept in safety; they had no powers in the disposition of the estate.

If no executor was appointed in the will, as was very common with spoken or nuncupative wills, then the task of distributing the assets would be assigned to the chief beneficiary, the widow of next-of-kin. This appointee was known as the administrator-with-will-annexed and the grant of probate on such a will was called an administration-with-will-annexed, abbreviated to AW in most records. He or she had exactly the same powers as an executor.

If the chief beneficiary was a child, then administration-with-will-annexed *durante minori aetate* would be granted to a responsible adult pending the child reaching his/her majority.

Provision made for family, friends and charities obviously vary with the individual, but there are certain patterns.

Let us start with charity, although it may not seem that most useful part of the will to the family historian, it may provide clues as to a testator's origins and to his interests and connections. A city dweller's bequest to a country church, for instance, may tell you where he grew up. He may have left money to the school or university he attended or benefit the trade or profession he belonged to by endowing apprenticeships.

The giving of money to the church and other charities was something which was regarded as a strong moral obligation, reinforced by tradition and the exhortations of the clergy. Charitable bequests were a vital part of the pre welfare state 'social service fund'. The commonwealth was kept afloat by such bequests, which helped eke out the poor law contributions and keep the poor from starving in times of economic distress.

The medieval custom had been that a married man's personal estate had to be divided in three ways; one third went to his widow, one third to his children and the remainder for his 'soul's part'. Early wills reflect this, with the final third going to pay for the testator's entry into heaven by funding church candles, masses, vestments, bells and the like. Later on these sort of bequests were replaced by gifts to schools, to the parish poor, to set up apprenticeships and to provide a 'dowry' for 'poor maids'. When Shakespeare died, £2 was the usual sum given to charity in wills.

Widows' rights over their husbands' estates were protected. It was not in the interests of the state to have numbers of indigent widows 'thrown on the parish'. As we have seen, the ancient custom was that she was entitled to one third of her husband's personal estate, and also one third of his landed property as her dower. If wife and children were not properly provided for in a will they could apply for a common law writ to get their entitlement.

Over the years testators were gradually released from the obligation to provide for their families by a series of laws, enacted in the seventeenth and eighteenth centuries. A father could now 'cut his son off with a shilling', at least as far as his personal estate was concerned (but see p. 28). He could also leave his wife to fend for herself, in theory.

Hardly anybody ever did and for those few hard done by widows, there would be a good chance of them winning a case at equity if they were brave and rich enough to engage in litigation.

The widows of yeomen, gentry and above were, by now, usually provided for by a marriage settlement which made sure that they had somewhere to live and an income after their husband's demise. Wives of farm workers and the like would have the security of being allowed to live in their copyhold cottage until they died or remarried.

The overwhelming majority of men provided for their widows, and indeed for common law wives. A Marlborough clothier, John Walford, who died in 1616, left all his property to Agnes Surley 'now the wife or called, taken and reputed to be the wyfe of mee'. In the same year the female servant of a man from Climping in Sussex, appointed his sole executrix, took the will to court and won the right to her 'employer's' copyhold.

The usual pattern for a married man's will, from the fifteenth to the nineteenth century, was that he left his main property to his eldest son, either sole or in conjunction with the widow until she died or remarried. Younger sons might be provided for with lesser holdings or, more often, with a lump sum or annuity payable by the heir and chargeable on the real estate. Unmarried daughters would be given cash for their dowry and some household goods.

If there were no sons, daughters would inherit.

Wills which benefited a man's children were accounted 'privileged' and stood a good chance of going through probate even if they were not properly executed.

You should be wary of making the assumption that all children are referred to in the will, this is normally the case. If any of the children were married by the time their father died, no mention may be made of them if settlements had been made for them at the time of their marriage.

Women's wills often concern themselves with the household and personal things which were theirs to dispose of. Items such as their 'childbed linen' and pieces of jewellery are often carefully left to a daughter or niece.

Landladies and nurse keepers are frequently the chief beneficiaries or even executrices in bachelor wills. Sailors, who left wills more than most ordinary working men, often left their back pay, their sea chest and few belongings to a kindly or unscrupulous woman who had looked after them in their last illness.

Ties of blood and affinity were more highly regarded than they are now and most testators left some small legacy or memento to their brothers and sisters and other close relatives, it might be just enough to buy a mourning ring.

Godchildren were usually remembered in wills and there are invariably small bequests to favourite servants. Dr Johnson left the bulk of his estate (worth about £1500) and an annuity of £70 to his loved black servant, Frank. One of his executors regarded this as 'ostentatious bounty and favour to negroes'.

Silver plate, pewter items, watches and books are often specifically bequeathed, as are pieces of furniture. Admittedly it was rare to leave your wife nothing but your second-best bed, as Shakespeare did, but beds and their 'furniture' (bedclothes) were valuable possessions.

Clothes were relatively much more expensive and prized than in these days of mass production, and cloaks, coats gowns and even shirts and underwear might be left to relatives or friends. Many men had a special attachment to their sword and made sure it went to a good home.

There are a number of misunderstandings that can arise when reading a will if you are not familiar with the law and terminology of the time. Some historians have given undue significance to the wording of preambles without, perhaps, realising that there were set forms which the local attorney would use. The creation of entails has been seen as an indication of extreme concern for the preservation of family property when it was very much the usual procedure. People have assumed that the omission of a child from a will indicates that he or she was a 'black sheep' when he or she was, in fact, provided for by some sort of a property settlement at an earlier stage.

Perhaps most confusing for those who are unfamiliar with probate records are the descriptions of relatives. The terms son- or daughter-in-law usually meant stepchildren, for instance. True sons- or daughters-in-law may be referred to simply as sons or daughters. The word cousin may denote any sort of relative. Shakespeare described his granddaughter as his niece! So be careful.

Similarly, 'cutting off with a shilling' is not necessarily what it appears. The legal authority, William Blackstone, said that it was a 'vulgar error', commonly made, that 'cutting off with a shilling' had any validity in English law. Isaac Burnel, who died in 1820, told his solicitor that he had left one shilling to all his relatives to prevent their trying to overthrow his will, which was in favour of his illegitimate children. The solicitor explained that there was no need. Nevertheless, many lawyers still advise their clients to do it and it is a phrase which crops up regularly.

The bequest of a shilling in a will can indicate a variety of things. The heir-at-law or a married daughter might be left a shilling by way of noting that they had already had settlements made on them, and they had not been forgotten. Thomas Short of Hagston in Buckinghamshire, who died in 1720, left his eldest son a shilling 'by reason that I have given him a portion already'.

Sons-in-law were frequently 'cut off with a shilling' without there being any necessary implication of animosity or distrust. It was just a 'coded message' which meant that the legacy the testator had left was for his daughter's own use. If the father was really suspicious of his son-in-law, he would leave his daughter's legacy in trust, adding a priviso that she should only receive the capital if she was widowed.

If 'cutting off with a shilling' is indicative of a parent's dislike of a child, then there is usually no doubt about it. Johan Jacob Vesenbeck, a wealthy eighteenth century seal maker, gave his son one shilling and 'cut hem off for ever for hes extream wickednes to me'. His will favoured his other son whom he regarded as being in danger of being starved by his unkind mother (or stepmother). Left to her tender mercies, Vesenbeck reckoned, the boy would 'schüt so small as a mouse'.

WHAT DID YOUR ANCESTOR LEAVE?

For grants of probate and administration made since January 1858, you will find a valuation of the estate, including real property, in the margin of the indexes at Somerset House. For the earlier period, when the Church Court dealt with the matter, there may be problems.

The will is not necessarily a reliable guide as to what assets the testator actually had when he died. He may have left legacies of a hundred pounds here and a hundred pounds there, but his estate may have been encumbered with debts which ate it all up.

If a will was made some time before death, the testator's circumstances may have changed.

As has been explained above, the will maker may have been in possession of real estate which does not feature in the will at all.

There are various ways of finding out what his assets really were; the most informative and reliable is probably via Death Duty records (see below, pages 34—39), which started in 1796. There are some other sources which may give you some idea of his financial status.

For wills proved and letters of administration granted from the mid-sixteenth century to the end of the first quarter of the eighteenth century, there may be an inventory and, much more rarely, an account. Sadly, virtually no inventories for PCC probates, the wealthiest and thus most interesting testators and households, survive before 1661 (perhaps burnt in the Great Fire of London), though there are indexes now to the c. 30,000 for the subsequent half-century (including Izaac Walton, whose inventory ends, 'fishing tackle and other lumber'). However, the picture is very different in the local courts where they are to be found in great quantity for almost a century before the Civil War and continuing, like PCC, to the early eighteenth century; though there is a tendency for post-Restoration inventories to summarise the value of the contents without itemising them as inearlier decades. Depending on the arrangement of the records, the indexes to wills and admons. sometimes, but not always, include inventories (should be indicated in Gibson's *Probate Jurisdictions*).

The executor or administrator was required to provide the court with a detailed list and evaluation of the deceased's goods. Many of these inventories survive and they usually include a room by room description of everything in the house, a list of money owed and owing, with debtors and creditors named, details of leases, stock-in-trade and farm animals.

Using an inventory, you may be able to construct a complete picture of a forbear's residence, including such details as the colour of the curtains, the books on the shelves and the pots and pans in the kitchen. You may even find out what sort of bonnets your x-times great grandmother wore.

The account of how the executor or administrator had dealt with the estate had to be rendered within a year of the grant of probate or administration. Very few accounts survive but, when they do, they can be very informative, itemising all the expenses incurred in the winding up of the estate, including travel expenses and bills for meals, etc. The total given at the end is more realistic than that in the inventory as it deducts the executor's/administrator's expenses, which might be considerable, particularly if he had to engage in litigation.If you are researching a seventeenth century family, it is well worth enquiring at the record office to see if an inventory or even an account survives.

As has been explained above (see p. 14), all administrators and some executors were required to enter into a bond. Bonds usually approximate to the value of the estate; in some cases they are double it.

In some courts, the Prerogative Court of Canterbury being a case in point, a register of probates and of administrations was kept. In

John Wise. On the first Day Administration of all and singular the goods Chattels and Credits of John Wise late of the City of Oxford Bachelor deceased was granted to Edward Bigg the Uncle and only next of kin of the said Deceased having been first sworn by Commission duly to administer

Sub £1000

Sept

Mar

Charles Wroughton. On the seventh Day Administration of all and singular the Goods Chattels & Credits of Charles Wroughton formerly of Warwick Street Holborn in the County of Middlesex Mariner) but late of Calcutta in the East Indies Bachelor deceased was granted to Susanna Wroughton Spinster the natural and lawful Sister and one of the next of kin of the said Deceased having been first sworn duly to administer

Sub £100

Sept

Mar

Sir James Watson. On the seventeenth Day Administration of all and singular the Goods Chattels and Credits of Sir James Watson Knight late one of the Persons Judges of the Supreme Court of Judicature at Fort William in Bengal in the East Indies deceased was granted to Dame Joanna Watson Widow the Relict of the said Deceased having been first sworn duly to administer

Sub £3000

Sept

Mar

Page of an eighteenth century Prerogative Court Administration Act Book showing the English version, with valuation of the personal estate given in the margin (Public Record Office PROB 6/176).

31

the PCC, these are called Probate Act Books and Administration Act Books. From the late eighteenth century a valuation of the estate is given in the margin. Remember that it only covers personal estate *within the province of Canterbury*.

None of the above include real estate. To find out what your ancestor's freehold house was worth may be a problem. Records of conveyances are difficult to trace (see p. 22) and until Death Duties were levied on real estate, the best way of getting some idea is probably through Land Tax records, which date from 1780 and are mostly held in county record offices (see J.S.W. Gibson, M. Medlycott and D. Mills, *Land and Window Tax Assessments*, Federation of Family History Societies, Birmingham, 1993).

For copyhold properties, you should consult manorial records (see p. 22).

IS THERE ANY OTHER DOCUMENTATION WHICH SURVIVES APART FROM THE WILL OR ADMINISTRATION (INVENTORIES AND ACCOUNTS)?

For grants made since January 1858, it is worth making application to Somerset House to see if a case file has been kept.

Apart from the inventory, account, bond and possibly entry in an Act Book described above, for most church probate courts little else survives in the way of 'paper work' supporting a grant, unless there were complications, except, of course, Death Duty records. These are dealt with in the next section.

If the estate became the subject of litigation or scrutiny, there may be a whole range of fascinating material.

You will usually get wind of complications when you go through the will and administration indexes or calendars. If they are the original indexes used by the court officials, then a law suit over an estate will often be noted with the words 'by sent(ence)' or 'by decr(ee)'. This means that the will/administration was disputed. In the case of a will, it may mean that it was 'propounded'.

Propounding, otherwise known as 'proof in solemn form or form of law', was a process used to establish the authenticity of a suspect will. Maybe it was not properly signed or witnessed or it might just have been that the executor anticipated opposition from some member of the family and wanted to make his claim extra firm. Once a will had been propounded, it was more difficult to contest it than if it had been proved in 'common form' (by the executor's oath alone).

Propounding involved the examination of witnesses and if the evidence they gave survives, it may add a great deal to the family story.

If there was a full law suit, then all sorts of revealing records may be available. Probate litigation might be handled in the minor courts, but it was often passed on to the senior courts, those of the Archbishops of Canterbury and York. The records are, therefore, now to be found in the Public Record Office (for the Prerogative Court of Canterbury) or the Borthwick Institute (for the Prerogative Court of York). The addresses for both are given on p. 19.

As the years passed, there was an increasing tendency for the London court (the Prerogative Court of Canterbury) to handle probate suits. Only there, in Doctors' Commons, as it was known, was there a body of expertise.

The church courts, from the sixteenth century, dealt with suits over the authenticity of wills, disputes as to who should be appointed administrator and actions 'in inventory and account'. These last were a way of defrauded legatees calling the executor or administrator to account. They were a way of obtaining some idea of the assets and were often the preliminary to a case at equity. The church courts had no powers to call in the assets, so if a beneficiary felt he had been done out of his legacy, he had to go to the king's court. It was, more often than not, the Court of Chancery.

If you are lucky enough to find probate litigation among the records of the prerogative or any other of the ecclesiastical probate courts, it is always worth checking to see if there was a Chancery suit subsequently or concurrently. Chancery not only handled the business of getting legacies paid, it also dealt with cases which involved real estate and the legality of the provisions of a will. If the relatives thought they could overturn a will by proving the testator was mad or drunk, then the case would go to the church courts as it was the validity of the document which was in question. If, however, a family thought it had grounds for preventing Uncle Joseph leaving everything to his nurse, then proceedings would commence in Chancery or another equity court.

The records of Chancery are in the Public Record Office. An explanation of what information they contain and instructions on how to search them are given in *Never Been Here Before?* by Jane Cox (Public Record Office, 1993).

The most exciting records emanating from probate litigation in the church courts are the evidence of witnesses, known as depositions or cause papers. The Doctors of Civil Law were very thorough and even minor squabbles about small amounts of money might involve the summoning of numbers of witnesses.

They were likely to be servants, relatives, neighbours and friends. Each was asked to give the examiner details of his age, address, connection with the deceased, occupation, etc. He or she would then be thoroughly questioned about the circumstances surrounding the making of the will and about the deceased's attitude to his nearest and dearest. It is sometimes possible, using these records, to piece together a full picture of your ancestor's family and social circle. Often, a vivid death bed scene is depicted and conversations repeated.

As well as the evidence of witnesses, there may be pleadings (called allegations or libels and answers), judgements (called sentences or decrees), registers of proceedings (called Act Books) and, perhaps the most interesting of all, exhibits. Diaries, letters, account books and even objects might be produced in court to prove a point. Cases known as 'interest causes', where relationship to the deceased had to be proved, often throw up pedigrees.

The records of Prerogative Court litigation are described in *Wills, Inventories and Death Duties* by Jane Cox (Public Record Office, 1988).

WHY ARE DEATH DUTY RECORDS USEFUL?

• They provide a central index to wills and administrations, to a limited extent (pre-1858).

• They provide information about the beneficiaries of the estate and the assets (after 1853 including real estate) which you may not find elsewhere.

Death Duties were first imposed in 1796 with the introduction of Legacy Duty. The records of the levying of this and other inheritance taxes are in 8000 volumes, registers and indexes spanning 1796 to 1904. They are kept in the Public Record Office, at present in the Chancery Lane building (Chancery Lane, London WC2A 1LR, Tel. 081 876 3444 and ask for the Rolls Room).

The indexes (classification: IR 27) are on microfilm, as are some of the registers (classification: IR 26).

A week's notice should be given if you wish to consult the registers for the period 1858–1904.

These records comprise one of the most useful discrete archives for historians of English and Welsh families.

Legacy Duty, imposed in 1796, was a tax on residues and legacies of personal estate only. It applied to money left in wills or passed as a result of grants of administration. Close relatives who inherited, namely wives, children and parents, did not have to pay duty and there is no reference to estates thus disposed of in the records. Remoter relatives had to pay a percentage of their inheritance. There was a sliding scale which started with brothers and sisters paying 2 per cent and went up to 6 per cent for distant cousins and 'strangers in blood'. Very small estates were exempt.

In 1805, Legacy Duty was extended to cover closer relatives and legacies and residues which were to be raised by the sale of real estate.

The 1815 Stamp Act extended the duty to all relatives except spouses.

In 1853, Succession Duty was introduced in addition to Legacy Duty. It covered any sort of property transfer which happened at death, even if there was no will or grant of administration. Thus transfers which were occasioned by the existence of a trust were taxable.

In 1881, Probate Duty was introduced. This was a tax on all personal property passing at death.

In 1884, Estate Duty superseded Probate Duty. Now, the tax was imposed on all property passing at death.

People domiciled abroad were exempt from all these taxes.

The scope of the taxes was gradually extended between 1796 and 1884. For the researcher this means that, until 1815, there is a much slighter chance of finding any particular individual than there is later on. Between 1812 and 1840, 598,811 estates appear in the registers. Bearing in mind that the population of the country in 1841 was 15,914,000, this is a very small percentage. After the introduction of Succession Duty in 1853, it was reckoned that 16 per cent of all deaths were represented by an entry in the Death Duty registers. Presumably that was 16 per cent of adult male deaths.

Using the Death Duty records as a central probate index

As we have seen, wills and administrations pre-1858 are scattered. The Death Duty indexes provide the nearest thing there is to a central index for these, although before 1815, only a small proportion of estates are included.

There are 605 volumes of indexes, in different series. For the period 1796 to 1812, there is a strictly alphabetical index prepared by the PRO on the open shelves in the search room. The indexes tell you in which court the grant was made and, using Gibson's *Probate Jurisdictions*, you can find out where the will or administration entry now is. The courts are referred to by means of abbreviations, such as PY for Prerogative Court of York. With the help of the Gibson guide, you should be able to work out what the abbreviations mean.

Using the Death Duty records to supplement what you have read in the will or grant of administration. 1796–1904

As the amount of Legacy Duty payable was determined by the relationship of the beneficiary to the deceased, the officials needed to identify those relationships precisely. The Death Duty registers are divided up into columns, one of which is headed 'consanguinity'. This is a gift to the genealogist as relationships are not always clearly defined in the will. It is particularly useful for identifying illegitimate children who may be classified as follows:

Stra NC = stranger, natural child
Stra ND = stranger, natural daughter
Stra NS = stranger, natural son

Someone just described as a cousin in a will may appear in the Death Duty registers as a DBM, descendant of a brother of a mother, and so on. An aunt will be classified as either an SF (sister of a father) or an SM (sister of a mother).

A full list of the abbreviations used in these records is given in *Wills, Inventories and Death Duties* by Jane Cox (Public Record Office, 1988).

Entries which relate to grants of administration are particularly useful. The church court and Principal Probate Registry records of an intestacy grant supply only the name of the administrator, whereas the Death Duty entry will tell you who the distributees were and how much each got. In the case of a married man with children, the Death Duty entry will give you the names and addresses of the children.

The true value of an estate may be found and, after 1853, totals will include the real estate. Also, specific valuations may be given for items bequeathed in wills, like the Stradavarius violin a professor of astronomy left a friend in 1796 and the Turners left by Lord Leconfield in 1880.

Many of the Death Duty entries have notes of letters sent out by the officials of the Board of Stamps in their attempts to collect the taxes. The first demand would issue at the time of probate, the second a year later and then, if there was still no response, subsequent letters would go out at three- and six-monthly intervals. If the beneficiaries who were liable proved difficult to get hold of, there may be addresses given for them over a period of years as the tax man chased them round the country.

Marriages may be noted in cases where legacies were contingent on marriage. If your great great grandmother came into £300 from her uncle's estate when she married your great great grandfather, then it would be taxed at the time of the marriage and the government would need to know about that event.

An example of how a Death Duty entry can fill out the family story comes from Victorian Chiswick.

In a house called 'The Cedars' lived an artist called Henry Dawson. In 1878 he died. One imagines the heavily curtained sick room and the hushed maids and nurses scurrying back and forth with whispers and potions. Later, the family would have assembled in the drawing room (widow, four sons and one daughter) and the lawyer would commence the reading of the will: 'In the name of God, Amen ...'

Henry Dawson's will can be inspected in one of the great Somerset House registers. It is a standard sort of document which leaves the widow Dawson a life interest in the estate and an annuity for the daughter. The Chiswick house and Dawson's two houses in Nottinghamshire and his Sussex farm were to be divided between the sons after their mother's death.

From the Death Duty entry, we learn that the widow survived her husband for only a year. The Nottinghamshire and Sussex properties were then sold off and one of the sons, William, stayed with his family in 'The Cedars'. An unmarried brother, a lithograph artist, occupied two rooms in the house. The real estate was valued at £6,000.

For the daughter, a 23 year old at the time of her father's death, there were some sad scribbled notes in the register. By 1908, she was in a lunatic asylum. She stayed confined until her death at the age of 86, maintained by her four brothers.

The series known as Reversionery Registers can be especially informative as they tend to span a long period of a family's life. The series was set up in 1899 to deal with outstanding Succession Duty claims going back as far as 1812.

Succession Duty was payable when money from trusts was transferred to the beneficiaries, even if the trust had been set up before the Succession Duty Act of 1853.

For instance, George Hall of Sprot(t)borough, Yorkshire set up a trust for his daughter, Sarah, at his death in 1833. The terms of the trust were that his property should be sold at Sarah's death and the money raised was to be given to her children.

The Reversionery Register entry takes us through 78 years of the family' life. We learn that Sarah married a doctor called Anderson and that they produced one child who they christened Tempest (a howling baby perhaps?). In 1889 they were living at 17 Stonegate, York. By 1911 the doctor was dead and his widow had 'retired' to the Esplanade, Scarborough.

Warnings about the records

Death Duty records are difficult to interpret and you would do well to have a copy of the will (if there is one) to hand when you are looking at an entry. You will need to consult *Wills, Inventories and Death Duties* (cited on p. 34) to understand the abbreviations used and the column headings.

The registers and their indexes are in a number of different series and you should make sure that you have the right section of the catalogues (labelled IR 26 and IR 27). They are divided up as follows:

Death Duty Indexes

	IR 27
PCC wills, 1796–1811	1–16
PCC administrations, 1796–1857	17–66
Country courts, wills and administrations, 1796–1811	69–93
Country court administrations, 1812–1857	94–139
PCC and country court wills, 1812–1858	140–323
Court of Probate PPR wills, 1858–1881	324–419
Court of Probate PPR administrations, 1858–1863	420–429
Court of Probate PPR wills and administrations, 1882–1903	430–605

		IR 26
PCC		
wills	1796—1811	1—178
administrations	1796—1857	179—286
Country Courts		
wills and administrations	1796—1811	287—437
administrations	1812—1857	438—534
Will Registers	1812—1881	534—3292
Intestate Registers	1858—1881	3293—3433
Will and Administration Registers	1882—1894	3434—4855
Reversionary Registers	1812—1852	4856—4867
Succession Registers	1853—1894	4868—6262
Succession Arrears Registers	1853—1894	6263—6283
Estate Duty Registers	1894—1903	2405 registers

Approximately 500 Estate Duty Registers and 11 Succession Duty Registers are missing.

In the later volumes there are a number of 'blank' entries, with just the name of the deceased given. This simply means that the estate was not of sufficient value to attract tax.

There are gaps in the registers for administrations between 1863 and 1881.

The files for the period 1904—1931 have been destroyed, as have the Death Duty copies of wills which were made, except those for Devon which are in the county record office.

RESEARCH TIPS

- Record offices do not permit the use of pens or biros. You should take pencils and a sharpener or a typewriter/word processor.
- In some record offices you may need to book. *Record Offices and How to Find Them* (J.S.W. Gibson and P. Peskett, FFHS, 6th edn. 1993) has maps and clear instructions.
- Wills may contain a good deal of detailed information, some of which may only become relevant in the light of subsequent research. Always buy a photocopy.
- Do not forget about administrations. In some county and diocesan record offices the administration indexes are separate from the will indexes. You may have to ask to see them.
- Always check to see if there is an index of probate inventories.

- When searching for a will, administration or Death Duty entry, search forward three years from the date of death. Occasionally probate may be delayed even longer, if there was a law suit or other complications.
- There are many published will indexes, notably those produced by the British Record Society. These and other indexes are noted in the guides mentioned on p. 18. Consult these indexes in your local reference library before going off on any expeditions.
- If you are out of the country, your best bet is to apply to a Mormon family history centre to get copies of wills and will indexes sent to you from Salt Lake City. The LDS Church has filmed many will collections. However, check the latest indexes of probate records in Gibson's *Probate Jurisdictions*, some of the Mormon microfilms may be of superseded indexes.
- The published will and administration indexes for the 1650s are an excellent way of tracking down a 'lost' family, as they include *all* grants that were made during that time.
- If you really cannot read and understand the document in front of you, as a last resort get a list of professional researchers from the archivist. But first, get a photocopy to take home. Buy a Guide to old handwriting (there are several helpful and inexpensive booklets available), and use that to help you understand the old way of writing some letters. Most are much the same, and once you get the hang of reading simple common words, you soon find you can read most of the others too. Old documents, so long as they are in English, look far more intimidating than they really are. If you belong to a local family history society, take the photocopy along to a meeting and ask someone to help you when you are stuck. Record office staff will be happy to help with the odd word, but it is only fair to make sure you have passed the elementary stage before asking for the experts' help. They rarely have time to go through a long document with you, but will be interested as well in specific problems.

GLOSSARY OF SOME COMMON PROBATE TERMS AND ABBREVIATIONS

Account	The executor's or administrator's account of the winding up of the estate.
Act	The endorsement on a will indicating probate has been granted, the record of a grant in an act book.
Act Book	Court book containing notes of probate business.
Administration (Admon.)	Letters of administration granted by the court when no will was made or could be found.
Administration with will annexed (AW)	Grant made on a will where there was no executor. Similar to a grant of probate (qv).
Administrator	Person authorised to distribute an intestate estate, usually the widow, next of kin or principal creditor.
Admon.	Administration (qv).
Ador.	Administrator (qv).
Advocate	The church courts' equivalent to a barrister.
Affidavit	Sworn statement.
Affirmation	Declaration made by Quakers instead of oath taking.
Allegation	Pleading in the church courts. Also called a 'libel'.
Answer	Response to allegation or libel (qv).
Archdeaconry, Archdeacon's Court	Normally the lowest of the ecclesiastical courts with testamentary jurisdiction. In larger dioceses there might be several, often co-terminous with counties, whilst just one might cover the whole of a smaller diocese. It was not unusual for the bishop's consistory court (qv) to appropriate this jurisdiction, or for a commissary (qv) to be appointed for an archdeaconry.
AW	Administration with will annexed (qv).
Beneficiary	Person entitled to some part of a willed or intestate estate or benefitting under the terms of a trust.
Bona Notabilia	A Latin term meaning considerable goods, technically worth £5 and more. When the deceased had *bona notabilia* in more than one jurisdiction, a will should have been proved in a superior court.
Bond	Usually refers to the security an administrator (qv) had to give before he was permitted to meddle with the estate.
Book debts	Debts noted in an account book.
Caveat	A legal instrument for stopping a will being proved pending a law suit.
Citation	A summons to appear before a court.
Codicil	Postscript to a will.

Commissary	A person who held authority or a commission to exercise jurisdiction on behalf of an archbishop, bishop or other dignitary.
Commissary Court	A court acting with delegated powers from the bishop, normally as a consistory court but in one archdeaconry only - in contrast to an archdeacon's court which was subject to the archdeacon.
Common form	The procedure for making a grant of probate and other business.
Consistory Court	The bishop's ecclesiastical court, with superior jurisdiction to an archdeaconry court (qv). Theoretically wills of testators with *bona notabilia* (qv) in two archdeaconries within the same diocese would be proved in the consistory court, and often the wills of clergy were reserved to it. In many dioceses it displaced the archdeaconry court entirely, or had jurisdiction over certain parishes exempt from the archdeacon's jurisdiction. In large dioceses powers were often delegated from the consistory court of the diocese to commissary courts (qv) acting in different archdeaconries. The consistory court would normally have jurisdiction during periodic visitations of the bishop to different archdeaconries, when the archdeaconry court would be 'inhibited' (qv).
Consols.	Bank stock.
Copyhold	A form of land tenure for tenants of manorial lords.
Curation, Curator	Guardian(ship) appointed by the court for an executor, administrator, legatee or litigant who was under age.
Dean (and Chapter)	Clergy who were members of a cathedral chapter, often with peculiar jurisdiction (qv) over parishes in the patronage of that cathedral.
DBN, *de bonis (non)*	*administration de bonis non administratis.* Grant made if the original administrator died before he finished his task.
Decree	Any sort of summons issued by the church courts. Can also mean an interim sentence.
Deposition	Witness's sworn response to examination.
Devise	Gift of real property by will.
Diocese	The district over which a bishop had authority.
Doctor's Commons	The home of the London church courts, including PCC.
Double probate	Separate grants made to two executors of a will, if there was some reason why they could apply at the same time.
Entail	A settlement of property on a designated series of owners. The most usual sort specified that land should descend to the eldest son or daughter, their children and so on down.

42

Execution (of a will)	The signing and witnessing.
Executor (exor.)	Person appointed in a will to carry out its provisions. An executrix is a woman.
Free bench	A widow's right to stay in the matrimonial home until death or remarriage.
Grant	Approval of the submission of the executor or administrator, denoting probate or letters of administration.
Guardianship	See 'Curation' and 'Tuition'.
Heir at law	Person entitled to inherit the deceased's real estate either by custom or entail (qv).
Heirloom	Some treasured item long attached to the estate which might be claimed by the heir at law as part of the freehold.
Honour	See 'Manor'.
Inhibition	The period during the visitation of a bishop to an archdeaconry when the archdeacon's court would be closed and probate business conducted in the consistory court.
Intestate	Someone who died without making a will.
Inventory	List of deceased's personal estate (qv). They were common in the later 16th and 17th centuries, but became much less detailed and frequent in the 18th century.
Jurisdiction	The area over which a court claimed the right to grant probate or letters of administration. Peculiars within this area would be exempt from the jurisdiction of the court concerned.
Legacy	Gift made by will.
Letters of administration	See 'Administration'
Libel	Pleading in the church courts.
Liberty	See 'Manor'.
Manor	Occasional manorial courts had peculiar or exempt jurisdiction over a parish or part of a parish. An 'Honour' or 'Liberty' might be a group of manors with such exempt jurisdiction.
Messuage	Dwelling house and its land.
Nuncupative will	Spoken will, unsigned.
Overseer	Person sometimes appointed by will to help the executor by keeping the goods in safety.
PCC, PCY	See 'Province'.
Peculiar (Testamentary)	A parish or group of parishes, not necessarily adjacent or even in the same district or county, which were usually exempt from the testamentary jurisdiction of the archdeaconry and often the consistory court.
Personal estate, personalty, PE	Everything that a person possessed except freehold and copyhold land.

Portion	This may mean a marriage portion which a woman's family would provide or a child's entitlement to a share in his father's estate.
Prebend	A type of ecclesiastical peculiar.
Prerogative Court	See 'Province'.
Probate	The business of giving wills legal status. The word is also used to describe the court copy of the will with the grant of probate attached which was given to the executor.
Proctor	The church courts equivalent of an attorney or solicitor.
Proved	A will has been proved when a probate has been granted.
Province	The dioceses over which a archbishop has authority, ie, before 1858, in England and Wales, Canterbury (southern) and York (northern). The 'prerogative courts' of the arch-bishops had superior jurisdiction to all others, and Canterbury (PCC) was superior to York (PCY).
Pts., parts	Abroad.
Real estate, RE	Freehold and copyhold property, tithes, manors and advowsons.
Registers, Registered wills	Volumes of copy wills, made at the time of probate. It is these the searcher will normally see, though sometimes only original wills are available. These are not to be con-fused with archbishops' and bishops' registers, which record their provincial and diocesan activities, but also include occasional wills, particularly in medieval times.
Relict	Widow of the deceased.
Renunciation	When an executor declines to apply for probate.
Reversion	The returning of land to the original grantor after the term of the grant had expired.
Sentences	The final judgment on a disputed will, often entered in an act book (qv).
Settlement, strict	Eighteenth century method of entailing estates on heirs.
Surrogate	A deputy appointed by the ecclesiastical court to deal with testamentary and other matters.
Testament	Will of personal estate (qv).
Testator, testatrix (f.)	The author of a will.
Tuition	Guardianship over orphaned minors, under 15 (boys) or 13 (girls). See also 'Curation'.
Will	A written statement by which a person regulates the disposition of property and rights after his or her death, normally signed and witnessed. See also 'Testament'.